THE WEALTH CREATORS' MANUAL

A handbook for financial success

STEVEN SMITH, PHD

Wisdom Publishers

Copyright © 2023 Wisdom Publishers

All rights reserved

The characters and events portrayed in this book are fictitious. Any similarity to real persons, living or dead, is coincidental and not intended by the author.

No part of this book may be reproduced, or stored in a retrieval system, or transmitted in any form or by any means, electronic, mechanical, photocopying, recording, or otherwise, without express written permission of the publisher.

ISBN: 9798372495036
Imprint: Independently published

Cover design by: Art Painter
Library of Congress Control Number: 2018675309
Printed in the United States of America

This book is dedicated to individuals that crave financial success

Rich people believe 'I create my life.' Poor people believe 'Life happens to them.'

T. HARV EKER

CONTENTS

Title Page
Copyright
Dedication
Epigraph
Introduction

Chapter one: Understanding the role of money in society	1
Chapter two: Positive relationship with Money	3
Chapter three: Financial literacy	5
Chapter four: Budgeting and saving	7
Chapter five: The pitfalls of debt and how to avoid them	9
Chapter six: The role of debt in building wealth	11
Chapter seven: Building and protecting your credit	13
Chapter eight: Navigating the world of insurance	15
Chapter nine: The role of social class and privilege in financial matters	17
Chapter ten: The relationship between finances and mental health	19
Chapter eleven: Understanding and maximizing your income potential	21
Chapter twelve: Overcoming financial challenges and setbacks	23

Chapter thirteen: Understanding your money blocks and limiting beliefs	25
Chapter fourteen: Setting clear financial goals and creating a plan to achieve them	27
Chapter fifteen: Visualization and affirmations for attracting wealth	29
Chapter sixteen: Cultivating a wealth mindset and habits for success	31
Chapter seventeen: Embracing a healthy relationship with money	33
Conclusion	35
About The Author	37
Books By This Author	39

INTRODUCTION

The word "wealth" has long been associated with mystery and intrigue. But what exactly is wealth? Is it just the accumulation of wealth and material things? Or is there more to it than that? It turns out that everyone's definition of wealth is unique, therefore knowing your definition is essential to acquiring it. Wealth may be defined for some people in terms of their financial resources and their capacity to buy tangible goods. Others may be concerned with having the financial security and flexibility to live their lives as they like, according to their own terms. It might also be about being able to help others and have a positive influence on the world. And for many others, it's about feeling content and fulfilled in their lives. However, we choose to define wealth, one thing is undeniable: it matters. It matters for our societal standing, interpersonal relationships, and general well-being. It can offer us the means and chances to realize our ambitions, as well as a sense of stability and security in a frequently unstable environment. However, despite its significance, not everyone may readily acquire wealth. Hard work, discipline, and frequently a little luck are required. It necessitates thorough preparation and the readiness to accept measured risks. It also necessitates a thorough understanding of the numerous elements that go into building wealth, such as setting aside money for savings, investing, and paying off debt.

We shall explore the true meaning of wealth and why it matters in this book. We'll look at the numerous metrics for measuring wealth, including those that go beyond financial assets. We'll also discuss how money affects both our personal and professional life and how it may help us realize our ambitions. But acquiring material goods is only one aspect of riches. It is about enjoying the financial security and freedom to live the life we choose, according to our own standards. It is about being able to support our local communities and leave a lasting impression on the world. It is about experiencing happiness and fulfillment in our lives. Therefore, let's set out on this adventure together to learn what wealth really is and how to acquire it. Are you prepared to create wealth? "

CHAPTER ONE: UNDERSTANDING THE ROLE OF MONEY IN SOCIETY

The function that money plays in our daily lives is crucial to our civilization. It is a means of exchange that enables us to buy products and services, as well as a standard of value that enables us to assess the relative worth of various possessions. But money is more than just a means of exchange; it also has a rich cultural history that influences how we view and employ it. Over time, the idea of money has changed. Bartering was a common method of exchanging commodities and services in ancient societies, but it had its drawbacks because it required locating someone who had what you wanted in return for what you had to offer. Societies started adopting standardized items as a medium of exchange, such as shells or beads, to get around this restriction. These items might be used to buy other goods and services in addition to having worth in and of themselves.

The usage of money increased in complexity along with societies. Banks were founded to aid in the exchange of money and offer loans, and coins and paper money were introduced as a more practical way to trade value. Debit and credit cards are examples of digital forms of money that are available today and enable us to conduct transactions without actually exchanging cash. However, the function of money in society goes beyond only enabling transactions. It can be used to exercise power and influence, as well as a means of storing and transferring riches. Both stability and opportunity can be found in money, which can also be a cause of stress and strife. The norms and ideals of our culture and society influence how we view money. For instance, having a lot of money and material belongings is viewed as a sign of success and status in some civilizations, whereas it is viewed as shallow or even sinful in other societies. Our individual experiences and views might also have an impact on how we view money. In order to manage our personal finances and make wise choices about how we utilize and manage our resources, we must have a clear understanding of the function that money plays in society. Additionally, it can assist us in comprehending and navigating the more complex social and economic systems in which we currently reside. Therefore, let's explore the function of money in society in more detail and consider how we may use it to create a better future for both ourselves and those around us.

CHAPTER TWO: POSITIVE RELATIONSHIP WITH MONEY

Our relationship with money, which is a crucial aspect of life, can have a big impact on our happiness and overall financial success. A healthy awareness of money's function in our lives, as well as a sense of control and accountability over our financial decisions, are the foundations of a happy relationship with money. Stress, worry, and a lack of financial security, on the other hand, might be signs of a bad relationship with money. It could include bad practices like overspending, forgoing financial planning, or relying on debt to get by. Negative thoughts or experiences, such as a fear of failure or a lack of knowledge about efficient money management, can also have an impact on one's relationship with money.

How therefore can we develop a healthy relationship with money? Learning about money is a crucial first step. This entails comprehending the fundamentals of personal finance, including setting a budget, saving money, making investments, and handling debt. Learning about financial planning and comprehending the numerous financial services and products that are available to us are also part of it. Financial literacy is a lifelong journey, and there is always more to learn. Setting financial goals and making a plan to accomplish them is another essential component of a healthy relationship with money. This might include both short-term objectives like consolidating debt or setting up an emergency fund as well as long-term objectives like saving for retirement or purchasing a property. Making wise choices about how we use and manage our money can be aided by having a clear understanding of what we hope to accomplish financially.

Additionally, it's critical to be cautious of your finances. Instead of responding impulsively or skipping financial planning altogether, this is being present and conscious of our financial actions and their effects. Being mindful can include paying attention to our spending patterns and the effects they have on our overall financial well-being, as well as taking the time to consider our values and what is most important to us financially. A helpful tool is having a network of individuals you can chat to regarding money. This could be a support group, financial experts, or close friends and family. We may better understand our personal connection with money and how to create a positive one by talking about our experiences and asking for advice from others. Financial savvy, goal-setting, mindfulness, and a strong support system are all necessary for a healthy relationship with money. The rewards - financial security, peace of mind, and the opportunity to accomplish our goals - are well worth the effort and commitment required along the way.

CHAPTER THREE: FINANCIAL LITERACY

Understanding fundamental financial concepts and principles is known as financial literacy, and it is a crucial ability for both personal and professional success. It entails knowing how to efficiently manage our money, make wise financial decisions, and establish future plans. Having a good understanding of finances has several advantages. It can assist us in maximizing our earnings and available resources, avoiding financial pitfalls and scams, and achieving our financial objectives. It can also give us a sense of empowerment and control over our financial lives, which can result in more stability and security in our money.

Financial literacy is more crucial than ever in the complex and quickly evolving financial environment of today. It is necessary for navigating the many financial services and products we have at our disposal, including credit cards, loans, and investments. Understanding the bigger economic and social structures in which we live, such as the stock market and the function of taxes is equally crucial. Sadly, financial literacy is not often included in the classroom, and many people lack even a basic understanding of money matters. Inadequate financial planning, excessive spending, and dependency on debt are just a few examples of how this can cause financial stress and troubles. It's never too late to start learning about personal finance, which is fantastic news. We may improve our financial literacy by using a variety of resources, including books, websites, and financial specialists. The more we learn, the better prepared we will be to make wise financial decisions and succeed financially. It is a lifelong journey.

CHAPTER FOUR: BUDGETING AND SAVING

In order to achieve financial security and stability, budgeting and saving are vital components of personal finance. A budget helps us prioritize our spending and saving by outlining how we will distribute our income and resources over a specific time period. On the other hand, saving is the act of putting money aside for future goals or requirements and is a crucial step in creating financial security and preparing for unforeseen costs or emergencies. Saving money and sticking to a budget have many advantages. Making the most of our income while maintaining control over our spending and avoiding debt is possible with the use of a budget. It can also assist us in setting and achieving financial objectives, such as paying off debt or saving for a down payment on a house. We can live within our means and make wise financial decisions by using a budget as a tool.

On the other hand, saving is a crucial strategy for enhancing financial security and making preparations for the future. It can give us the means to reach our long-term financial objectives, like retirement or home ownership, as well as the ability to weather financial storms like a job loss or unforeseen bills. Making and following a budget can be difficult, particularly if we have several expenses or erratic income. Tracking our expenditures can help us find areas where we can save money or make adjustments. It's crucial to keep our spending in perspective and to provide room for flexibility.

Saving money can be difficult, particularly if we have numerous expenses or other financial commitments. But it's crucial to make an effort to save anything, even if it's just a little bit. Establishing a saving habit, even in little amounts, can be a crucial step toward achieving financial independence. In order to achieve financial security and stability, budgeting and saving are vital components of personal finance. We can use a budget to manage our spending and make the most of our income, and we can use savings to provide us the means to reach our long-term financial objectives and plan for the future.

CHAPTER FIVE: THE PITFALLS OF DEBT AND HOW TO AVOID THEM

For many people, debt is a normal aspect of life, and it can be a helpful instrument for funding investments or purchases. If a debt is not effectively handled, it can also be a source of stress and financial problems. A key component of personal finance is knowing how to avoid the dangers of debt. Taking up too much debt or debt that we cannot afford to repay is a common debt problem. Overspending, a lack of financial planning, or a failure to comprehend the conditions of a loan or credit agreement can all contribute to this. It might also be brought on by unanticipated costs or a change in our financial situation, like a job loss or an urgent medical situation.

Failure to make payments on time is another financial trap. This might result in late fines, increased interest rates, and harm to our credit rating. Additionally, it may result in creditor proceedings like a repossession or legal action, which might have very negative financial and legal repercussions. The dangers of debt can be avoided in a number of ways. Being aware of our spending and refraining from overpaying or taking on more debt than we can comfortably payoff is a crucial first step. Additionally, it's crucial that we comprehend the conditions of any loans or credit agreements we get into and complete our payments on time.

Making an emergency fund is another technique to stay out of debt. This savings account is reserved for unanticipated costs or emergencies. When unplanned expenses arise, having an emergency fund can prevent us from going into debt and give us a financial safety net to get through difficult times. If we are having debt problems, it may be beneficial to seek the advice of a financial expert or a credit counseling organization. These resources can give us the information and instruments we need to manage our debt and get our finances back on track. Debt can be a helpful tool, but it's crucial to be aware of the risks and take precautions to prevent them. This can involve watching our spending, comprehending the conditions of any loans or credit agreements we sign, and setting up an emergency fund, among other things. If we are having debt problems, it may be beneficial to seek the advice of a financial expert or a credit counseling agency.

CHAPTER SIX: THE ROLE OF DEBT IN BUILDING WEALTH

Although it is true that excessive or badly managed debt can be a burden and result in financial issues, debt is frequently seen as a bad financial instrument. But debt can also help you accumulate money, particularly if you use it wisely and strategically.

Leverage is one method that debt can be used for wealth creation. Employing borrowed funds to purchase assets with the potential to yield returns larger than the cost of the debt is known as using leverage. Leverage can be used, for instance, to use a mortgage to buy a rental property that earns rental income because the property has the potential to increase in value and produce income over time. By using credit to make purchases that will eventually provide income or increase in value, debt can also be used to create wealth. Because a business has the potential to make profits and increase in value over time, using a small business loan to launch or expand it might be an example of employing leverage. The use of debt to increase wealth necessitates careful preparation and a thorough grasp of the dangers and potential rewards. It's crucial to remember the conditions of any debt agreements and to make sure we have the funds necessary to make payments on time.

When debt is utilized strategically and responsibly, it can contribute to wealth creation. For example, using leverage to invest in assets with the potential to produce returns or using credit to make purchases with the potential to generate income or appreciate in value over time. But it's critical to take the hazards into careful consideration.

CHAPTER SEVEN: BUILDING AND PROTECTING YOUR CREDIT

Your capacity to borrow money and gain access to financial products and services is significantly influenced by your credit, which is a reflection of your financial history and spending patterns. A crucial component of personal finance is credit building and protection, which can have a big impact on your financial destiny. The timely payment of your bills is a crucial part of establishing and maintaining good credit. Missed or late payments might lower your credit score and make it more challenging to obtain credit in the future. It's crucial to handle your debt sensibly and refrain from going overboard with your spending.

Making responsible use of credit is another component of establishing and maintaining good credit. This entails using credit in a way that shows you have good money management skills and only borrowing what you can afford to pay back. It's also critical to understand your credit utilization, which is the ratio between the credit you are using and the credit you have available. Your credit score may suffer if you have a high credit utilization rate. Regularly reviewing and correcting any inaccuracies or anomalies in your credit report is another strategy to protect and grow your credit. Credit bureaus create credit reports, which detail your credit history and usage patterns. As inaccuracies can have a detrimental effect on your credit score, it is crucial to make sure the information on your credit report is accurate. It is crucial to be aware of and guard against identity theft and credit fraud. This may entail taking security measures like creating strong passwords, keeping a close eye on your accounts, and employing caution when giving out personal information over the phone or online. A crucial component of personal finance is establishing and maintaining good credit. It includes keeping up with bill payments, managing your credit wisely, monitoring your credit report frequently, and guarding against identity theft and credit fraud. You may improve your financial situation and gain access to the financial resources and opportunities you need to accomplish your goals by establishing and maintaining good credit.

CHAPTER EIGHT: NAVIGATING THE WORLD OF INSURANCE

A financial tool known as insurance can assist shield us from the financial repercussions of unplanned occurrences like accidents, illnesses, or natural catastrophes. Even while insurance is not frequently considered a strategy for wealth creation, it can support wealth growth by guarding against financial losses and maintaining our financial stability and security. The protection provides against the financial repercussions of unforeseen catastrophes is one-way insurance can help wealth growth. In the event of a serious sickness, having health insurance, for instance, can help pay the expense of medical care and avert financial devastation. The cost of repairs or legal fees in the event of an accident can also be covered with the aid of automobile insurance. Insurance helps safeguard our financial stability and security by defending against financial losses, which can serve as a base for wealth building.

By giving us peace of mind and enabling us to concentrate on other areas of our lives, like developing a business or purchasing assets with the potential to increase in value over time, insurance can also help wealth growth. This enables us to seek chances and take financial risks that may not be possible if we are continuously concerned about unforeseen costs or financial losses. It is crucial to remember that insurance is just one element of a comprehensive financial plan and is not a guarantee of wealth building. The conditions and exclusions of insurance coverage, as well as any deductible or co-payment demands, should also be understood.

By defending against financial losses and maintaining financial stability and security, insurance can contribute to wealth growth. Additionally, it might bring us comfort and free us up to concentrate on other facets of our lives that might aid in generating riches. But insurance is only one element of a thorough financial strategy, so it's crucial to pick the coverage that best suits our individual needs and circumstances. Getting Around the Tax and Estate Planning World

CHAPTER NINE: THE ROLE OF SOCIAL CLASS AND PRIVILEGE IN FINANCIAL MATTERS

The access to financial resources, opportunity, and security for a person can be significantly influenced by social class and privilege. Social class is the classification of people based on their socioeconomic standing and is often influenced by elements like money, income, occupation, and education. The degree of access to financial resources, opportunity, and security varies widely between socioeconomic classes. For instance, people from higher social classes might have more access to financial knowledge, credit, and investment opportunities than people from lower social classes, who might only have a limited number of these options available to them.

The unearned advantages or benefits that a person may have because of their socioeconomic status, color, gender, sexual orientation, or other variables are referred to as privileges.

The financial possibilities and consequences that individual experiences can be significantly impacted by privilege. Someone with racial advantage, for instance, would find it simpler to get credit or a job, but someone without it might experience prejudice or other obstacles to financial success. Recognizing the influence of social class and privilege on financial issues is crucial, as is working to build a more inclusive and fair financial system. In addition to confronting our own privileges and how they could affect our financial chances and results, this might involve lobbying for laws and programs that support financial literacy and access for underprivileged groups.

An individual's access to financial resources, opportunities, and security can be significantly impacted by social class and privilege. A more equal and inclusive financial system can be developed by recognizing and addressing these problems.

CHAPTER TEN: THE RELATIONSHIP BETWEEN FINANCES AND MENTAL HEALTH

The management of our finances can have a big impact on our mental health. Money and mental health are strongly related. On the other hand, having a good grasp of our financial situation might be impacted our mental health. Financial stress and anxiety are some ways that money can harm one's mental health. Money worries, such as stressing about bill payments or not having enough funds, can lead to stress and anxiety, which can have an adverse effect on our mental health. Mental health illnesses like depression or anxiety disorders might develop as a result of financial stress. However, mental health problems can also have an effect on our financial stability. Effective money management can be more challenging when we have mental health issues, which can result in issues like overspending, trouble budgeting, or late payments. It's critical to understand how money and mental health are intertwined and to take proactive measures to handle both well. This may entail obtaining professional assistance for mental health issues and financial advice for budgeting and money management.

Additionally, it's critical to consider how money affects our mental health and to put our mental health first when making financial choices. This could entail taking measures to lessen financial stress, like making a budget, establishing financial objectives, or getting financial education. The management of our finances can have a big impact on our mental health. Money and mental health are strongly related. Recognizing this junction and taking action to handle it properly is crucial. Examples include asking for professional assistance when necessary and putting our mental health first when making financial decisions.

CHAPTER ELEVEN: UNDERSTANDING AND MAXIMIZING YOUR INCOME POTENTIAL

Understanding your qualities, skills, and experiences and utilizing them to pursue financial possibilities are key to maximizing your economic potential. Additionally, it entails being proactive in looking for new income prospects, bargaining for fair pay, consistently learning new things, and increasing your abilities to boost your marketability. Assessing your abilities and skills is one technique to comprehend and optimize your earning potential. This can involve determining your strengths as well as the subject areas in which you have knowledge or competence. You can find possible income options that fit your abilities and skills by studying them.

Being proactive in looking for new revenue options is another approach to increasing your earning potential. This can entail networking and forming connections with people in your sector, keeping abreast of job openings and market developments, and pursuing professional development opportunities to boost your qualifications and marketability. It's crucial to bargaining for appropriate wages when looking for new employment prospects. This can entail investigating industry norms, realizing the worth of your abilities and knowledge, and having self-assurance.

To maximize your earning potential, it's critical to continually learn new things and improve your existing abilities. This can entail looking for possibilities for professional growth, such as training or education, or it can entail developing new talents through hobbies or side projects. Understanding your talents and skills, being proactive in looking for new income prospects, bargaining for fair compensation, and consistently learning and expanding your skills are all necessary to maximize your income potential. You may raise your marketability on the job market and pursue financial alternatives to boost your income by following these methods.

CHAPTER TWELVE: OVERCOMING FINANCIAL CHALLENGES AND SETBACKS

There are various ways to overcome financial difficulties and setbacks, however, the following methods might be useful:

• Establish a budget: You can find areas where you can make modifications or cut back by having a comprehensive picture of your income and expenses.

• Cut costs: Look for ways to reduce your expenditure by canceling pointless subscriptions or memberships, settling accounts, or reducing discretionary spending.

• Increase your income: If you can, look into finding ways to take on extra job or locate freelance or gig work as a way to make more money.

• Look for financial aid: If you're in need of money, there may be services that can help you get back on track. For advice, look into government assistance programs or consult a financial counselor.

• Plan ahead: Create a strategy to deal with any debts you may have and other financial difficulties you may be experiencing. It might also entail working with a financial advisor to develop a strategy for long-term financial stability.

Keep in mind that getting out of financial difficulties requires time and effort, but you can do it if you're persistent and have a strategy in place.

CHAPTER THIRTEEN: UNDERSTANDING YOUR MONEY BLOCKS AND LIMITING BELIEFS

Unconscious thought patterns like limiting beliefs and money blockages frequently prevent us from reaching financial success. Try the following to comprehend your own financial limitations and restricting beliefs:

• Consider your earlier experiences: Consider any financial experiences or messages from the past that may still be influencing your views today.

• Be mindful of your inner dialogue: Take note of your money-related ideas and beliefs, and whether they are positive or negative.

• Recognize your anxieties: What financial-related fears do you have? Are you scared of losing, winning, or something else?

- Request comments: Ask for their opinion and discuss your beliefs with someone you trust. To assist you in identifying and resolving your financial obstacles, you can also think about working with a financial coach or therapist.

- Examine your assumptions: Spend some time challenging your money blockages and limiting beliefs when you've recognized them. Exists any proof to substantiate or disprove your beliefs? Do you have any examples in mind that go against your beliefs?

- You can attempt to overcome your financial obstacles and limiting beliefs by becoming aware of them. This will help you have a better relationship with money.

CHAPTER FOURTEEN: SETTING CLEAR FINANCIAL GOALS AND CREATING A PLAN TO ACHIEVE THEM

You can make progress toward your financial objectives by setting clear financial goals and developing a plan to achieve them. You can use the following steps to establish financial objectives and build a strategy to reach them:

• Choose your financial priorities: What are your top financial priorities? Do you wish to eliminate debt, save funds for a down payment on a home, or create an emergency fund?

• Be specific and measurable in your goals: Try creating a particular goal, such as "I want to save $10,000 in my emergency fund within the next year," rather than just declaring "I want to save more money."

- Create a schedule: When do you hope to reach your financial objectives? Regarding what you can complete in a specific amount of time, be realistic.

- Establish a budget: You can devote your funds to your financial objectives and keep on track by using a budget.

- Identify possible barriers: What could keep you from reaching your financial objectives? Think about how to solve or lessen these problems.

- Examine and revise your plan: Regularly evaluate your progress toward your financial objectives and, if necessary, make changes to keep on course.

It takes time and effort to set financial objectives and develop a plan to reach them, but it may be a worthwhile investment in your financial security.

CHAPTER FIFTEEN: VISUALIZATION AND AFFIRMATIONS FOR ATTRACTING WEALTH

Affirmations and visualization are two methods for manifesting your desires that involve engaging your imagination and encouraging self-talk. Some individuals think that affirmations and visualization might aid in attracting prosperity and abundance into their life. You can use affirmations and visualization to draw money in the following ways:

• Visualize your objectives: Every day, take a few minutes to imagine accomplishing your financial objectives. When you reach the desired amount of riches, picture every aspect of your life in detail.

• Employ affirmations. Every day, tell yourself affirmations that will help you. Say, "I am worthy of abundance" or "I am drawing money and prosperity into my life," for instance.

• Act with inspiration: Although affirmations and visualization are potent tools, action needs also be taken in addition to them. Find ways to get closer to your financial objectives and take action to achieve them.

It's critical to remember that affirmations and visualization are not a substitute for sensible efforts toward financial success, such as budgeting, investing, and saving money. However, a lot of people discover that employing these strategies may keep them motivated and laser-focused as they work toward their financial objectives.

CHAPTER SIXTEEN: CULTIVATING A WEALTH MINDSET AND HABITS FOR SUCCESS

Financial prosperity can only be attained by developing a wealth mindset and successful behaviors. A wealth mindset is a method of thinking that is concentrated on success, affluence, and prosperity. It entails holding the conviction that you are deserving of prosperity and that you are capable of attracting and generating wealth in your life. It takes letting go of limiting beliefs and unfavorable thought patterns that may be preventing you from having a wealth mindset. This can include ideas about your own worthiness or potential, as well as messages from society about success and money. You may make yourself more open to new chances and create the way for financial success by changing your mindset to one of abundance and opportunity.

Having a wealth mindset is important, but so is establishing money-supporting habits. This can involve routines like setting up and adhering to a budget, setting aside a set amount of money each month, or making investments in your own training and personal growth. The ability to actively seek out new opportunities to make money or increase your wealth is a crucial habit to develop. This may entail adding to your workload or creating a side business, making real estate or stock market investments, or looking for ways to boost your income through promotions or wage negotiations. Maintaining organization and keeping track of your income and expenses are two more habits that might help you achieve financial success. You may manage your resources wisely and move closer to your financial objectives by maintaining organization and being aware of your financial condition.

Discipline is a crucial habit to develop if you want to succeed financially. This entails resisting the urge to indulge in momentary pleasures or make hasty purchases and instead selecting choices that are consistent with your financial objectives. It takes time and effort to develop a wealth mindset and successful habits, but with commitment and self-control, you may move closer to your financial objectives. You can lay the groundwork for a profitable and joyful future by creating a mindset of plenty and prosperity as well as successful financial practices.

CHAPTER SEVENTEEN: EMBRACING A HEALTHY RELATIONSHIP WITH MONEY

To be financially well-off, one must embrace a positive relationship with money. This entails appreciating money's value while realizing that it is not the most significant component of your life. Knowing your financial condition well is one step in embracing a positive relationship with money. This entails maintaining a budget, tracking your income and expenses, and being conscious of your financial priorities and goals. You may manage your resources wisely and work toward your financial objectives by having a clear picture of your financial condition.

Being aware of your spending patterns is another component of having a healthy relationship with money. This entails refraining from overindulging or making rash purchases, as well as selecting actions that are consistent with your long-term financial objectives. You may strike a healthy balance between enjoying the results of your job and saving and investing for the future by being aware of your spending patterns. Having a positive attitude regarding debt is equally as crucial as being aware of your spending patterns. This may entail creating a strategy for timely and effective debt repayment as well as refraining from taking on further debt. You can minimize financial stress and lay a strong basis for financial prosperity by having a positive attitude toward debt.

Finding a balance between your employment and other responsibilities is a necessary part of adopting a healthy relationship with money. Prioritize and work for your financial objectives, but also make time for your loved ones, friends, and other significant elements of your life, such as your personal interests and hobbies. You may build a balanced existence that is both healthy and enjoyable by striking a balance between your employment and other facets of your life. In general, adopting a healthy relationship with money entails realizing that it is not the most significant component of your life but simultaneously appreciating and understanding its place in your life. You may lay the groundwork for financial success and well-being by developing a positive relationship with money.

CONCLUSION

Anyone trying to succeed financially and prosper has found the Wealth Creators' Manual to be a helpful resource. Readers have learned the value of adopting a healthy relationship with money, establishing a wealth mindset, and developing success habits through the numerous chapters and advice provided in this book. These methods and ideas have given people a strong base on which to build money and achieve financial security. The significance of establishing specific financial goals and developing a strategy to accomplish them is one of the book's main lessons. You can stay motivated and focused as you work towards your goals if you have a clear idea of what you want to achieve financially. Additionally, you can lay a solid foundation for financial prosperity by forming habits that promote financial success, such as saving a particular proportion of your income each month or maintaining financial organization.

Being financially successful also requires developing a wealth mindset. This entails changing your perspective to one of abundance and opportunity and feeling that you are deserving of success and riches. You can make room for new chances and create the path to financial success by letting go of restrictive beliefs and unfavorable mental habits. To be financially well-off, one must embrace a positive relationship with money. This entails appreciating the value of money while yet realizing that it is not the most significant component of your life. You may strike a good balance between your financial goals and other significant aspects of your life by being aware of your spending patterns, avoiding overindulgence or impulsive purchases, and having a positive attitude regarding debt. The "Wealth Creators' Manual" has, in general, offered insightful tips and methods for reaching monetary success and prosperity. Readers may take charge of their finances and work to build a future that is both financially secure and fulfilling by applying the advice provided in this book.

ABOUT THE AUTHOR

Steven Smith

Steven Smith holds a doctorate in Construction Management. He is passionate about personal success.